WHERE IS OZZY?

CREATED AT FANTOONS ANIMATION STUDIOS

Art Director: David Calcano and Marielina Obando
Written By: Eduardo Braun and David Calcano
Additional Writing: Eduardo Benatar

Illustrated and Colored By: Juan Riera, Jorge Mansilla, Alberto Belandria, Leo Assis, Ray Punxh, Lila Cruz and Larissa Rivero

Producer: Mariafernanda Fuentes
Executive Producer: Linda Otero
Book Layout Designer: Brett Burner
Edited By: Veronica Sinnaeve

Sales: info@fantoons.tv
www.fantoons.tv / Ozzy.com

Ozzy Osbourne. Where is Ozzy? © 2025 Fantoons LLC. All Rights Reserved.

Ozzy Osbourne. Where is Ozzy? © 2025 Monowise
Under License to Global Merchandising Services Ltd.

No part of this publication may be reproduced, distributed or transmitted in any form or by any means, electronic, mechanical, photocopying or otherwise, without prior permission of the author.

Printed in China. ISBN: 978-1-970047-35-6

Introduction

In our second Ozzy book, we throw the kitchen sink... and more! After creating Ozzy's first and only official coloring book, and inspiring thousands of fans to rejoice over art straight from the music's DNA, we spice up the hardcore fan humor and of course incorporate the talent of some of the greatest artists in the business, those here at Fantoons.

We painstakingly went through Ozzy's entire catalog to conduct "research" for this book... all while blasting his music throughout the studio. We've created double pages FILLED with easter eggs and color just for you, my friends and fellow fans. Now, you've gotta find the Ozzman himself across the many wardrobe and atmospheric changes of his career, and there's only one condition:

PLAY THE MUSIC...LOUDEEEER!

Share in the excitement with your friends and celebrate Ozzy's music as he's inducted into the Rock & Roll Hall of Fame as a solo artist. Always with a sense of humor... if anyone knows how to have fun, it is Ozzy Osbourne. I'll always remember the music, but man... Ozzy has given me so much laughter and joy; he has truly made a mark on all of us.

I hope you enjoy this book as much as we enjoyed creating it. Let's celebrate the man.

HELL YEAH!

David

NOTE FROM THE PRODUCER

Thank you to everyone who worked so hard on this book. Special thanks to Marielina Obando for her dedication to the art direction and to all the illustrators for their patience and incredible work. Big thanks to Eduardo Braun and Eduardo Benatar for helping select the best ideas. You've all contributed to making this book beautiful.

MAFER

OZZY OSBOURNE

WHERE IS OZZY?

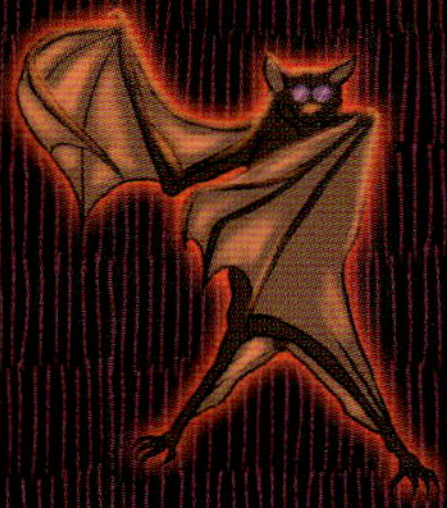
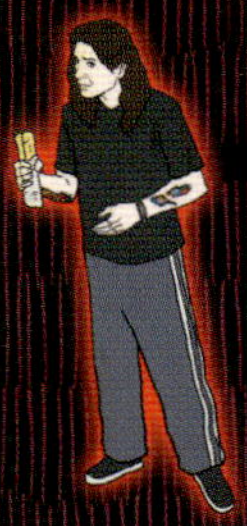
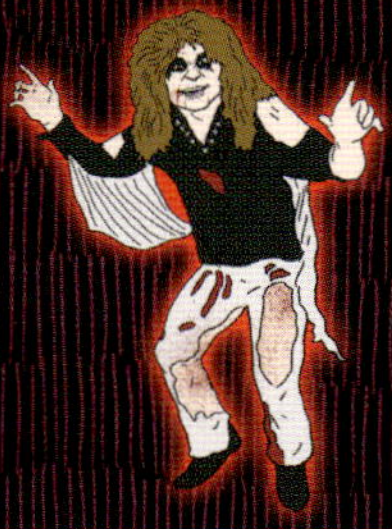
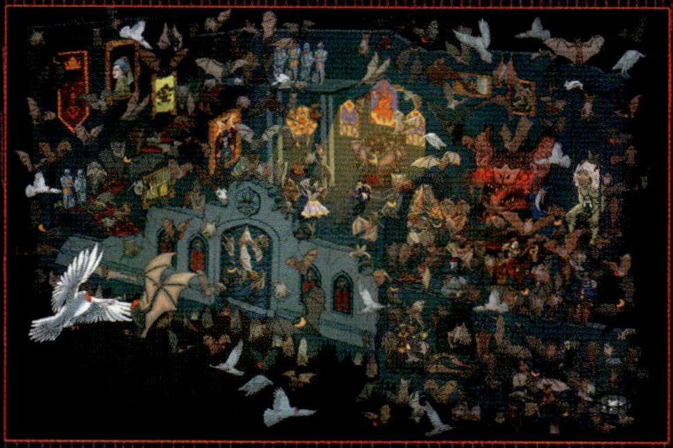
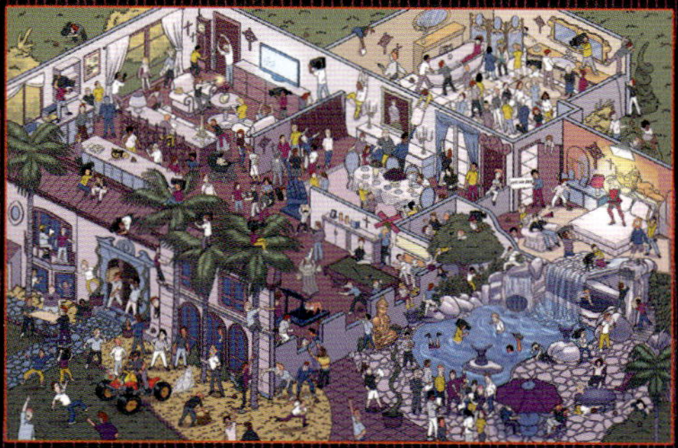
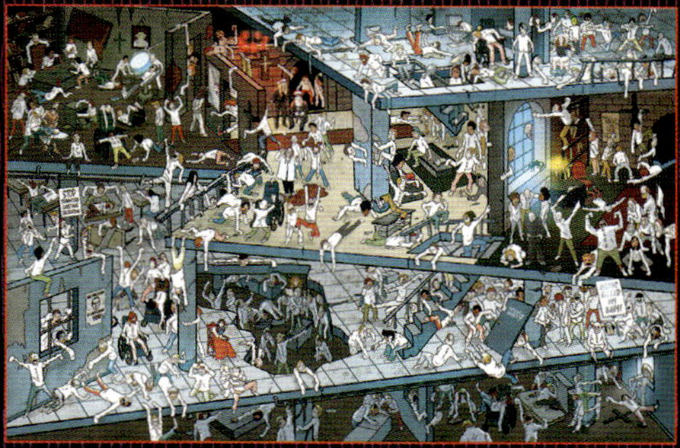
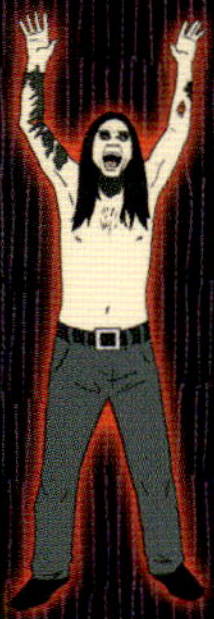
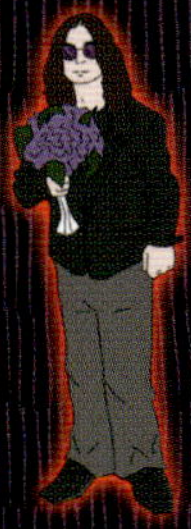
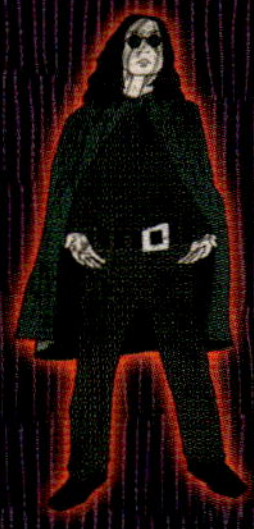
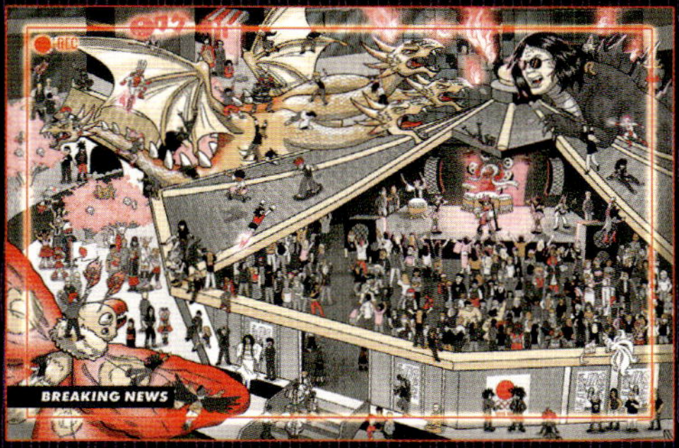
BREAKING NEWS
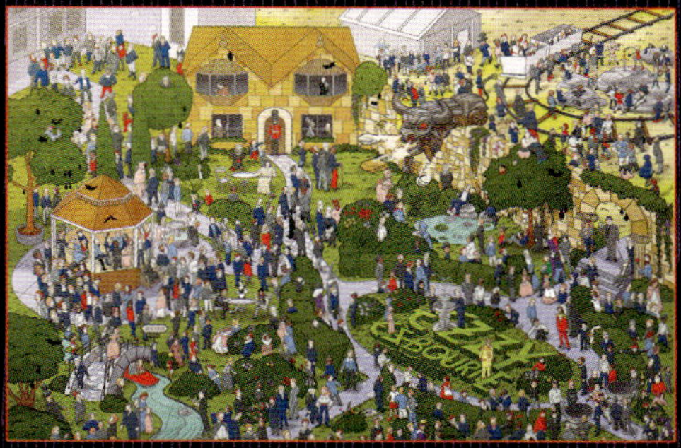
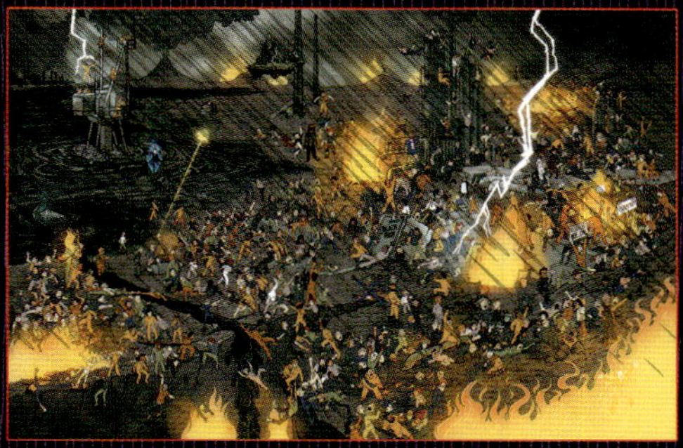
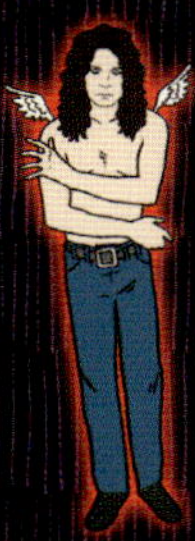
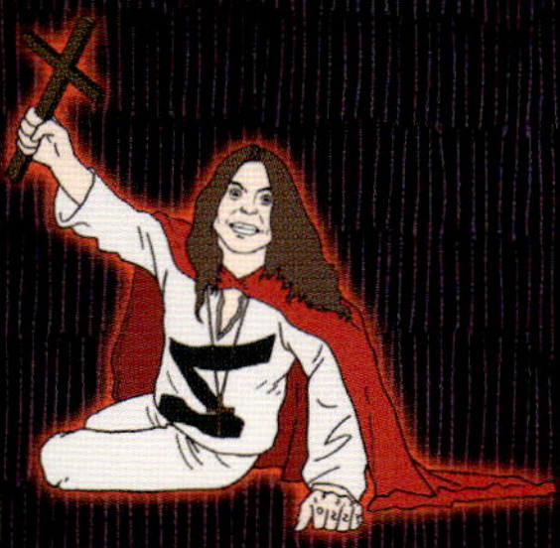
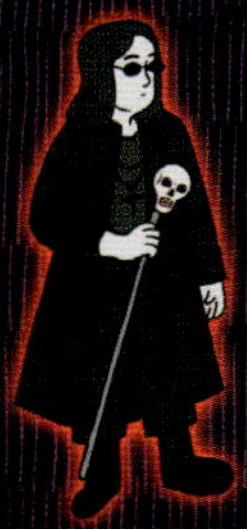
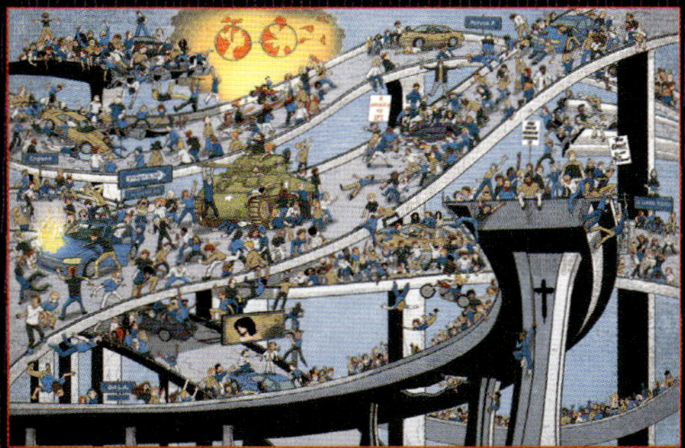
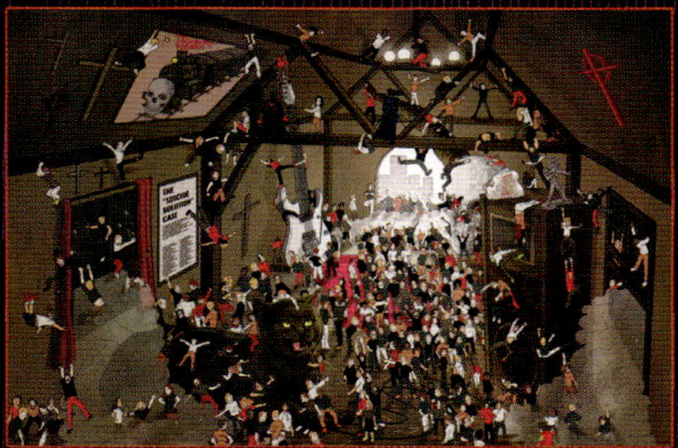
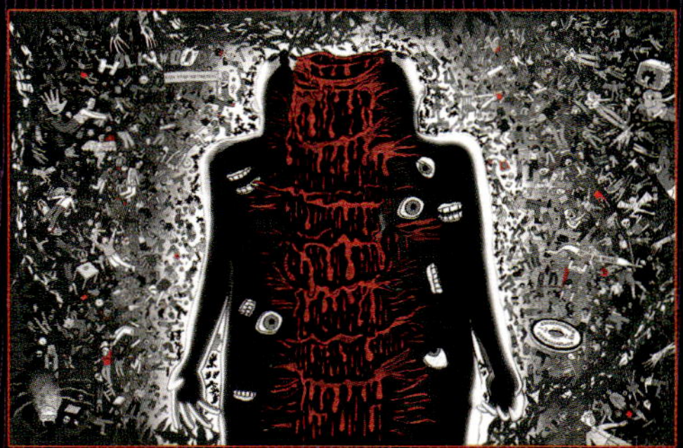

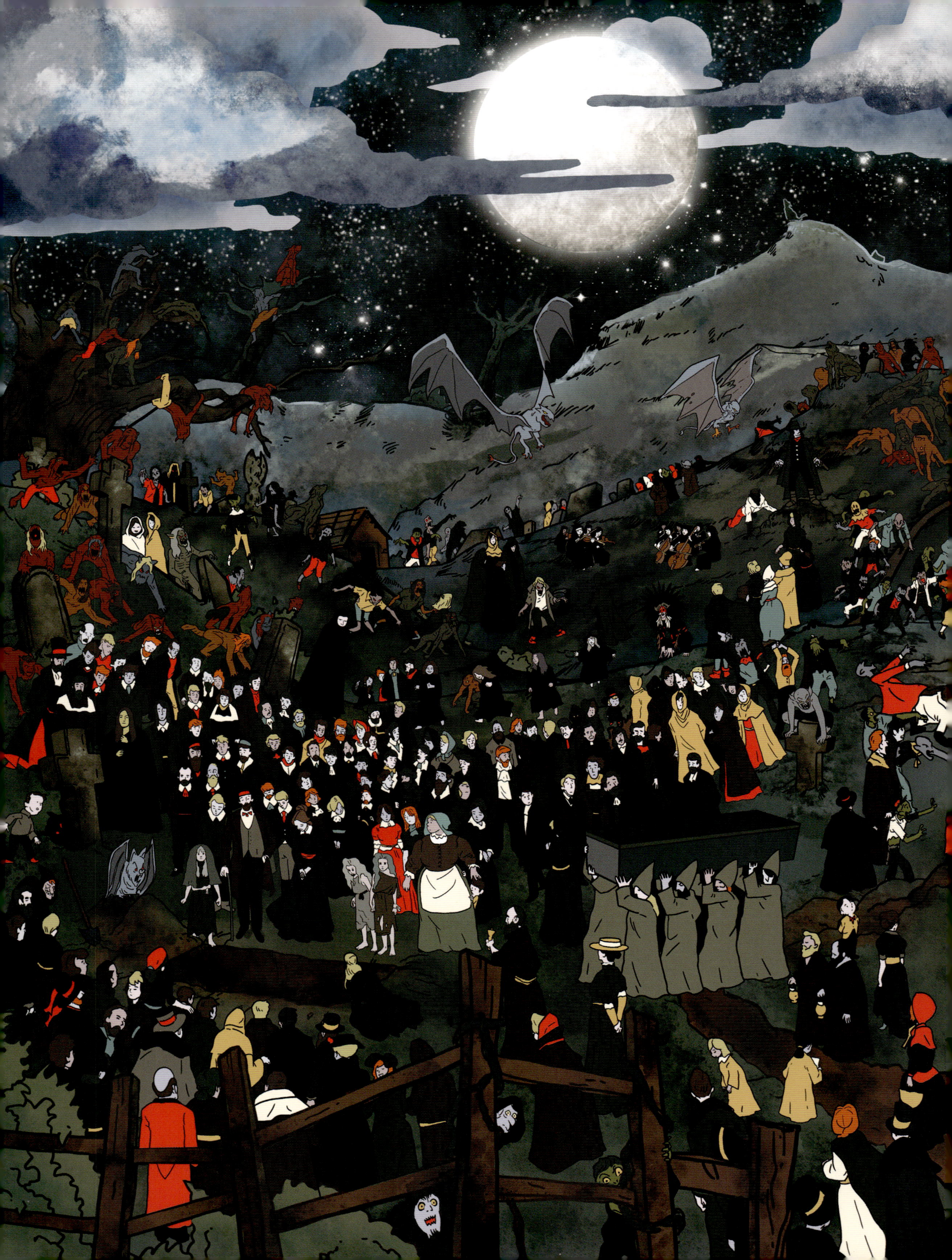

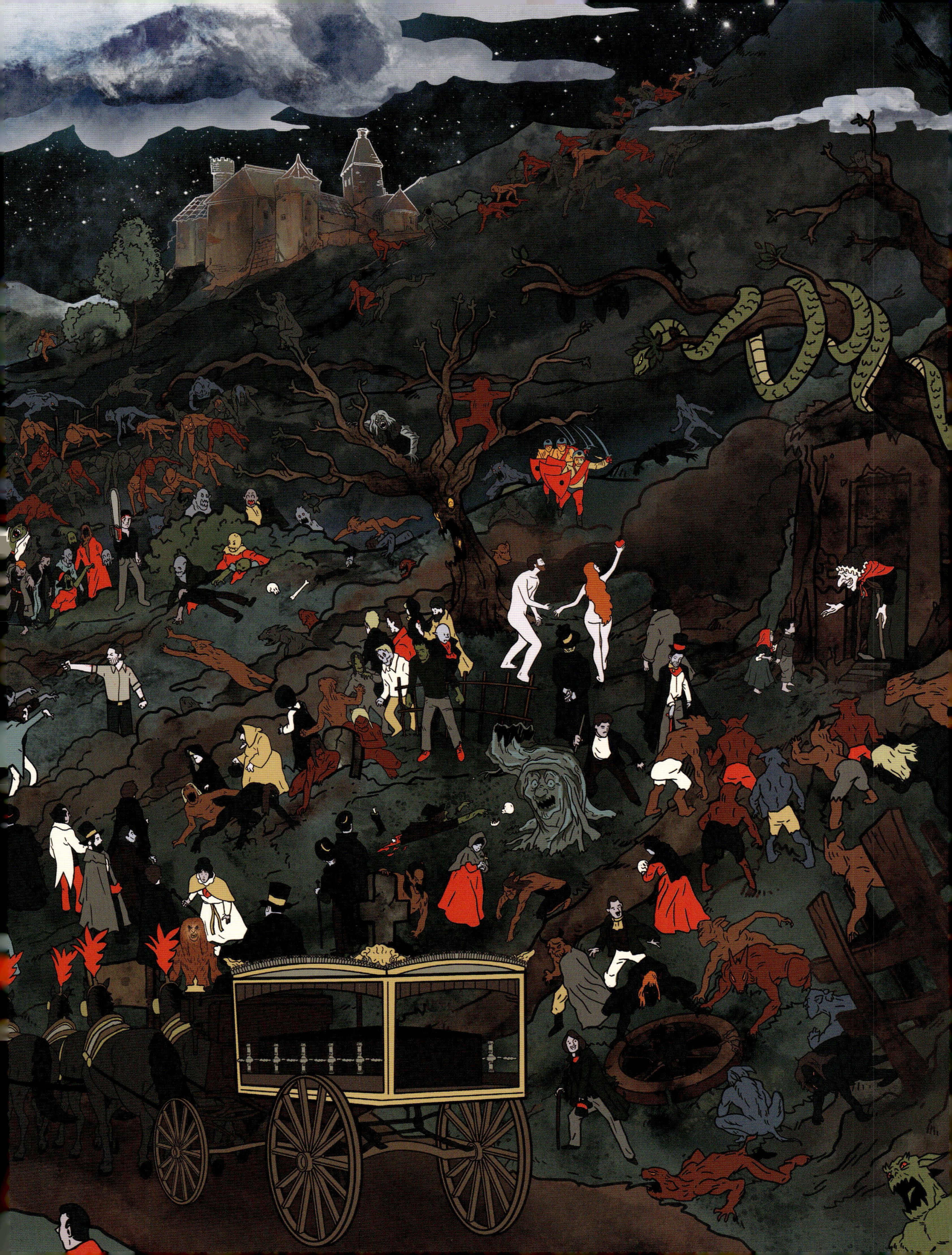

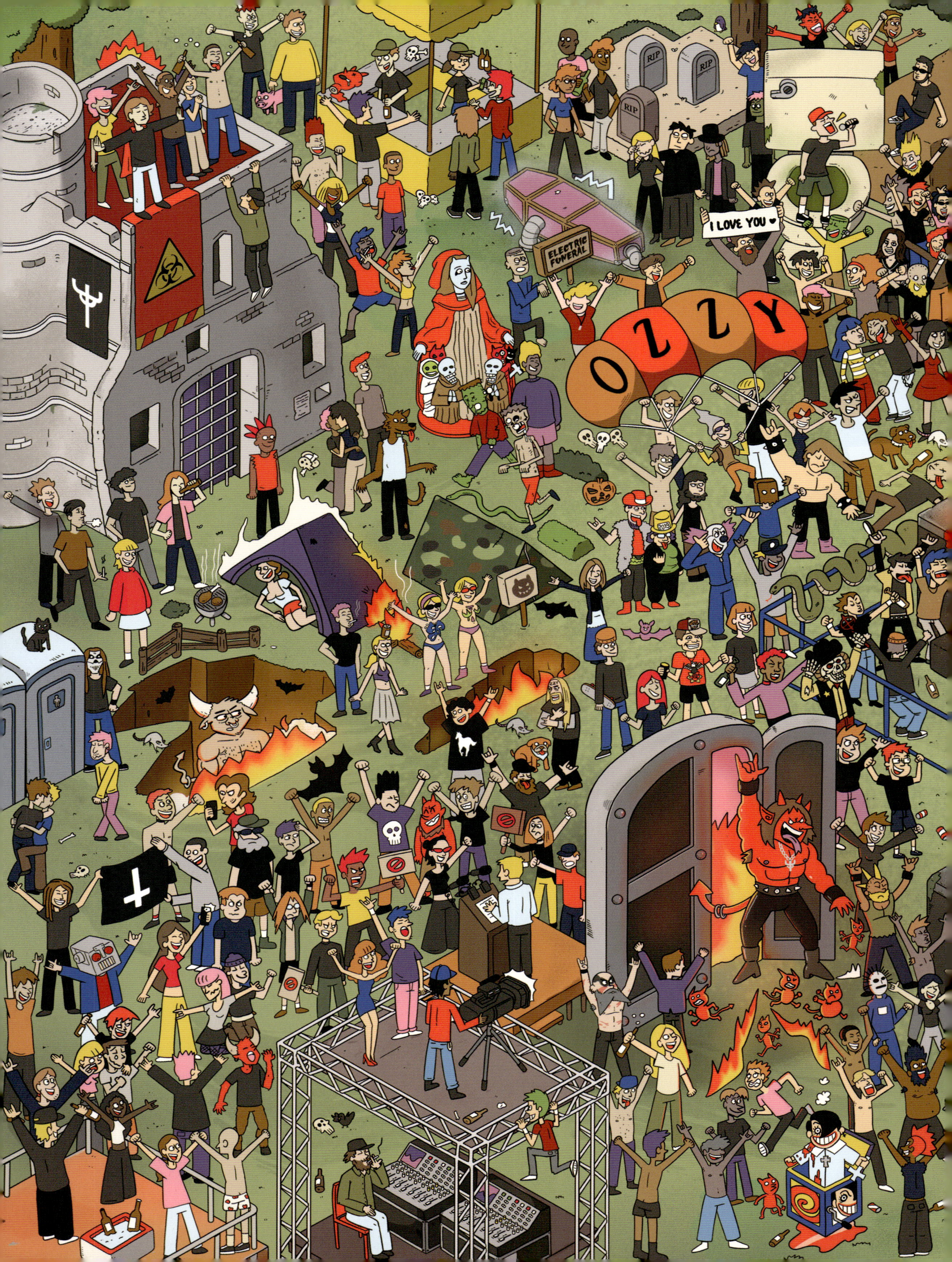
RIP
RIP
RIP
ELECTRIC FUNERAL
I LOVE YOU ♥
OZZY

OZZY IS OUR GOD! OSBOURNE
OzzFest
OZZFEST
OZZY
RIP
RIP
FUCK LOLLAPALOOZA

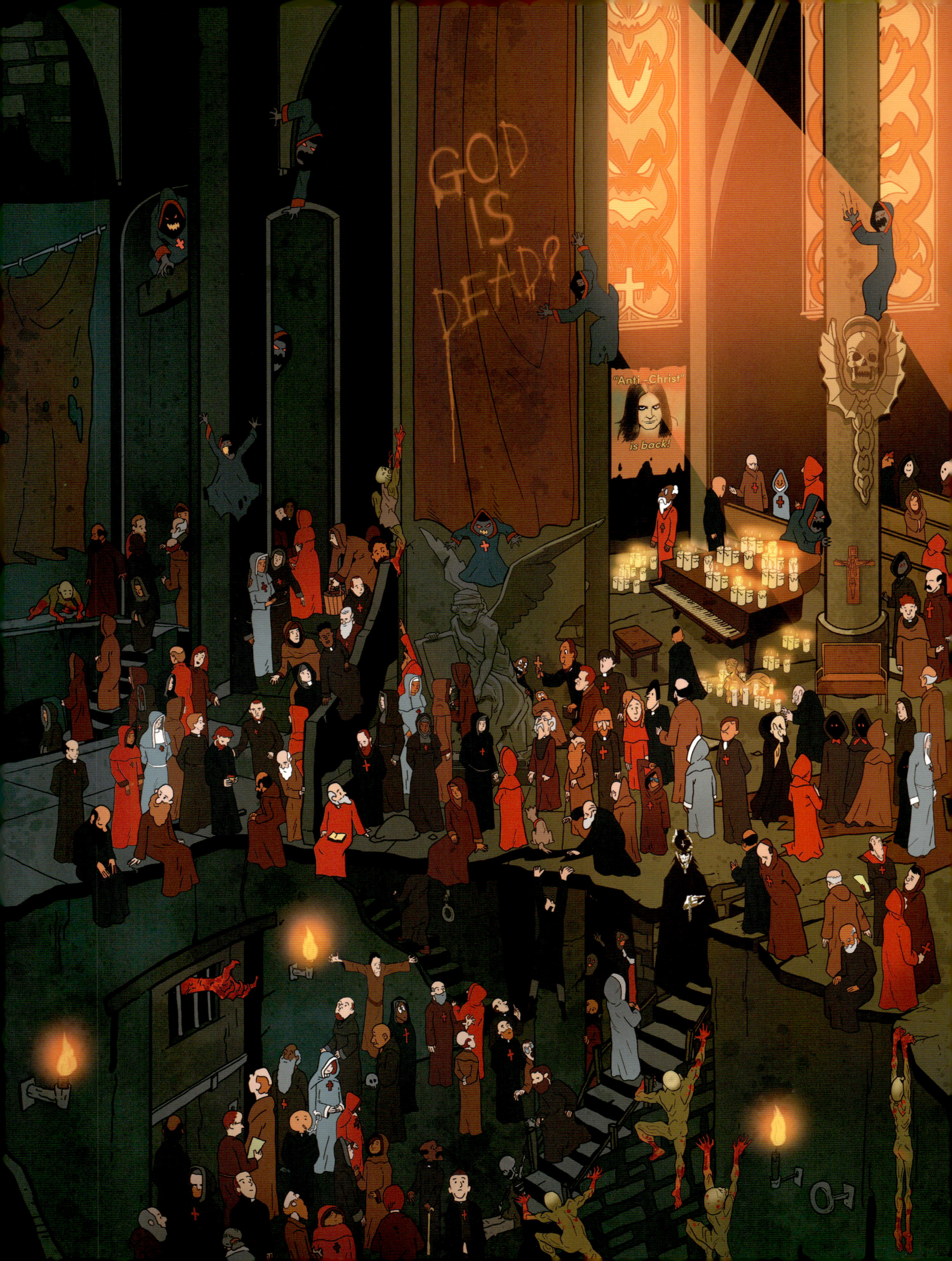

GOD IS DEAD?
"Anti-Christ"
is back!

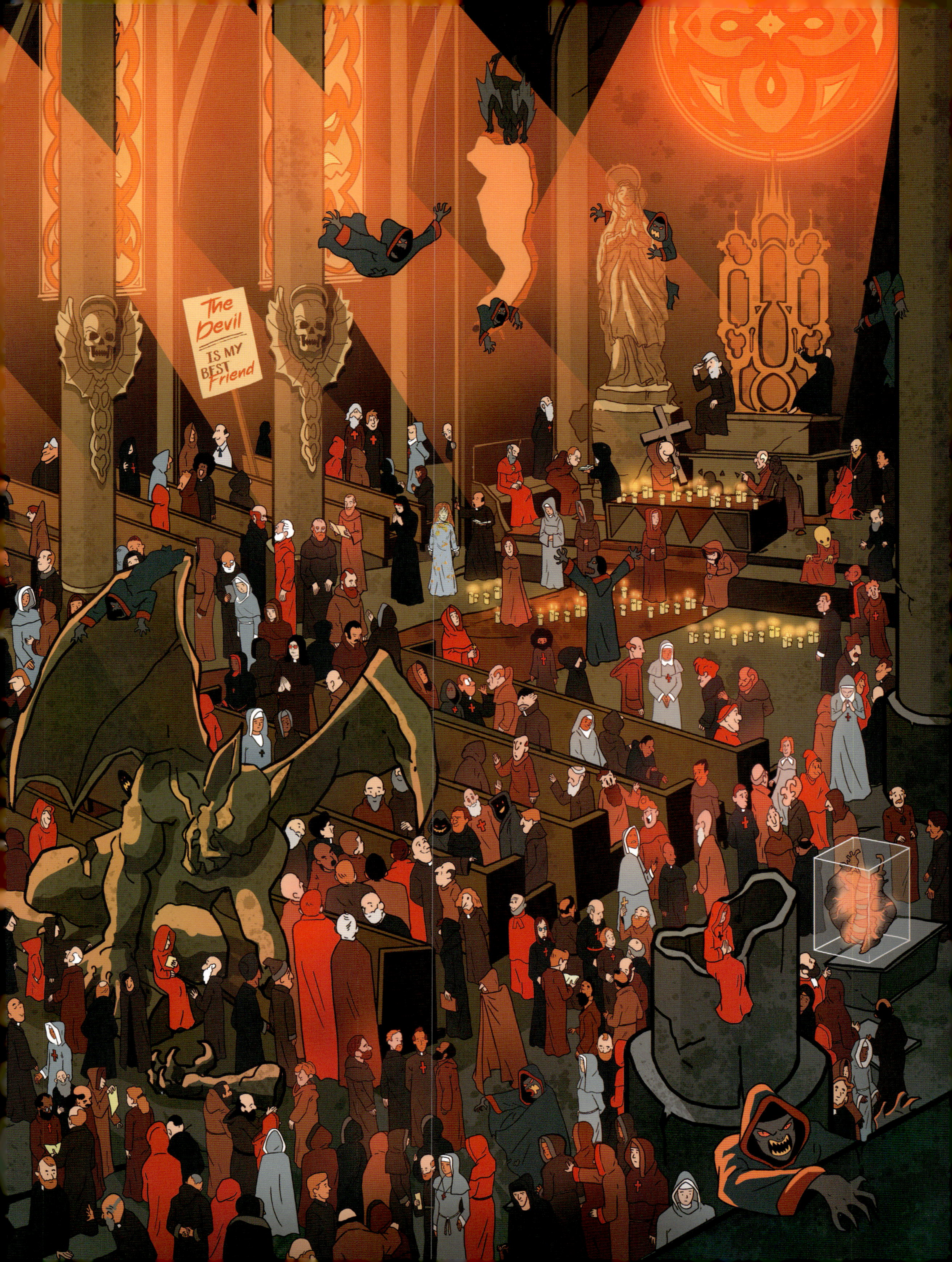
The Devil
IS MY
BEST
Friend

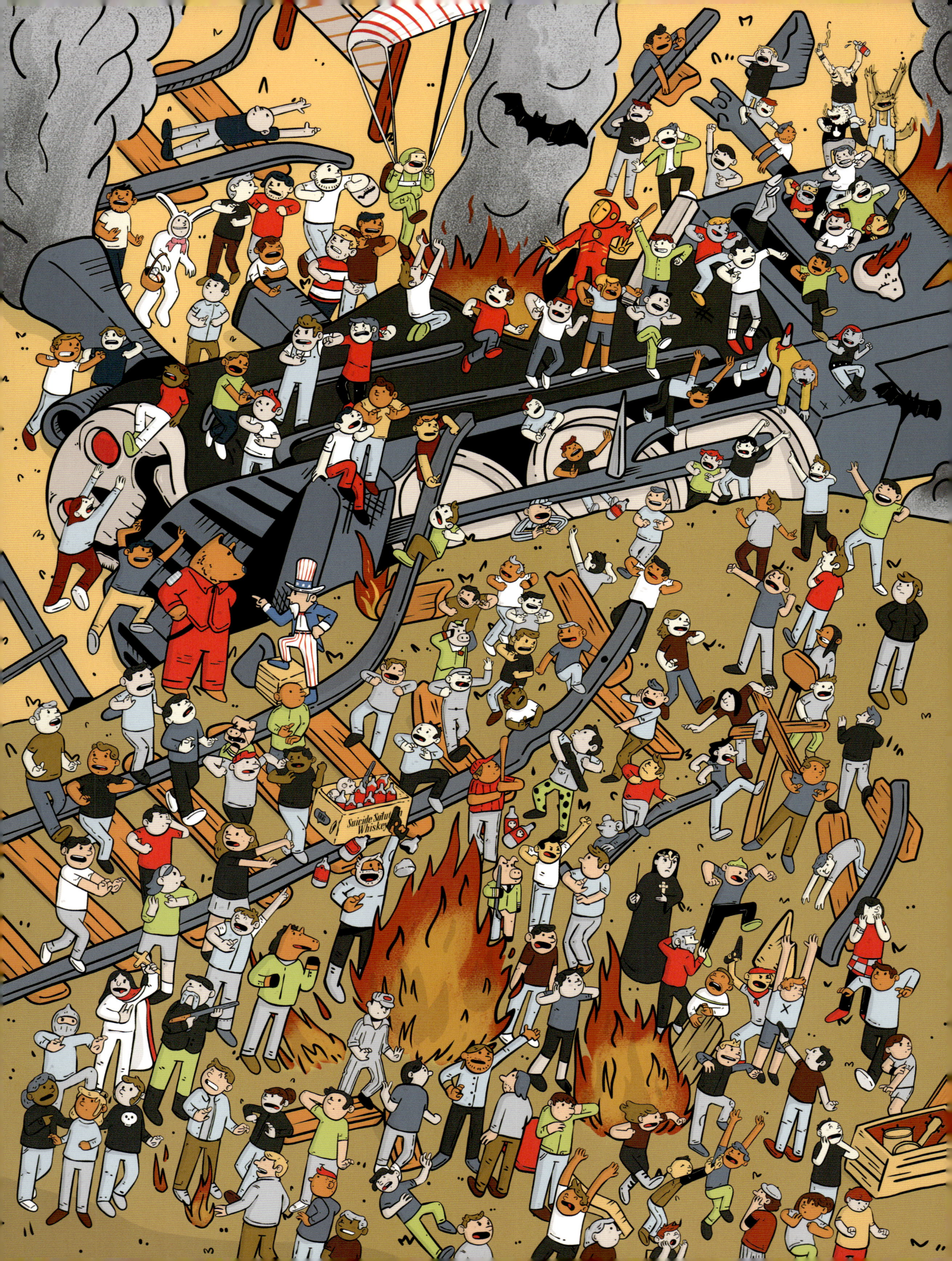
Suicide
Whiskey

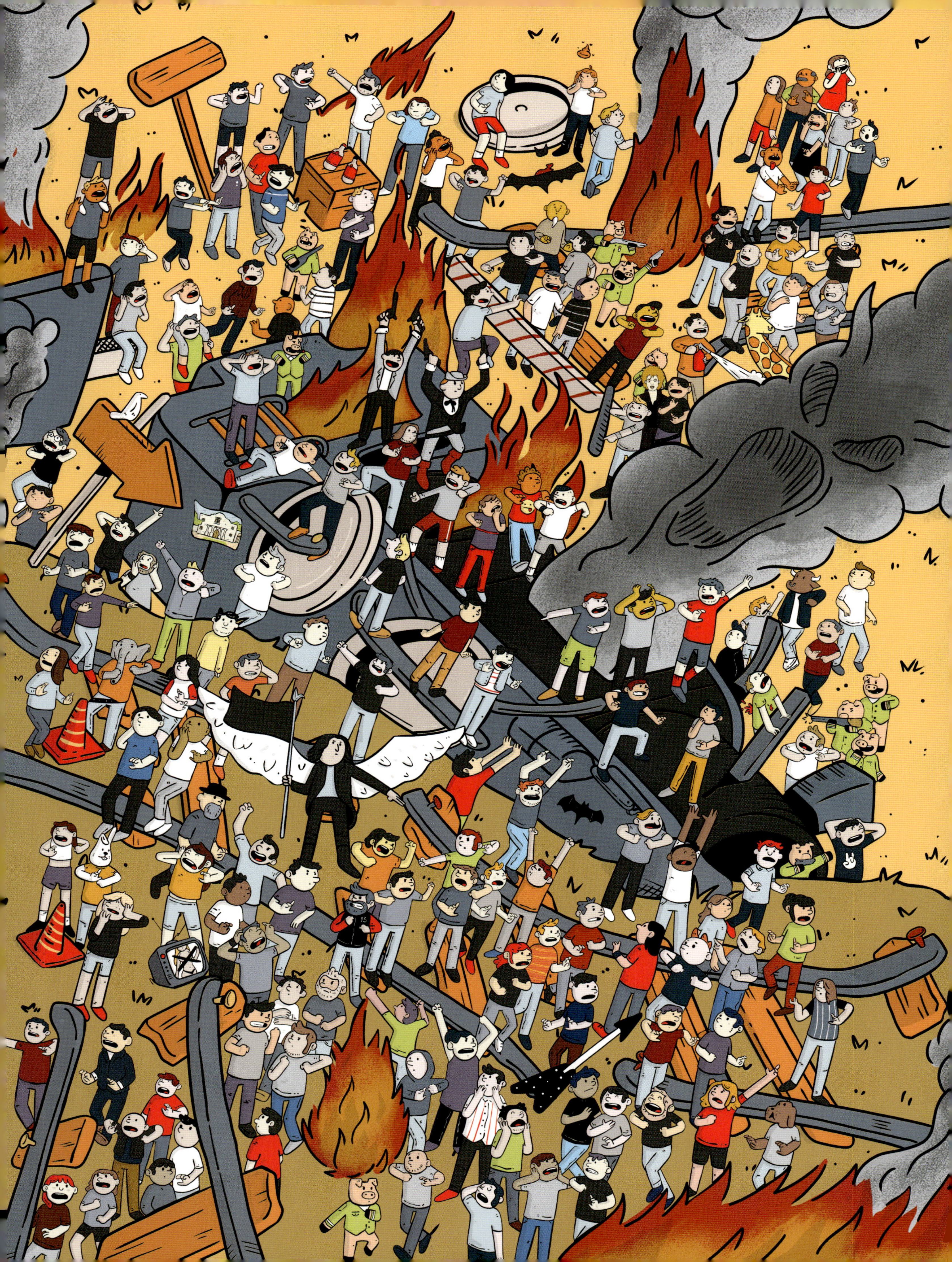

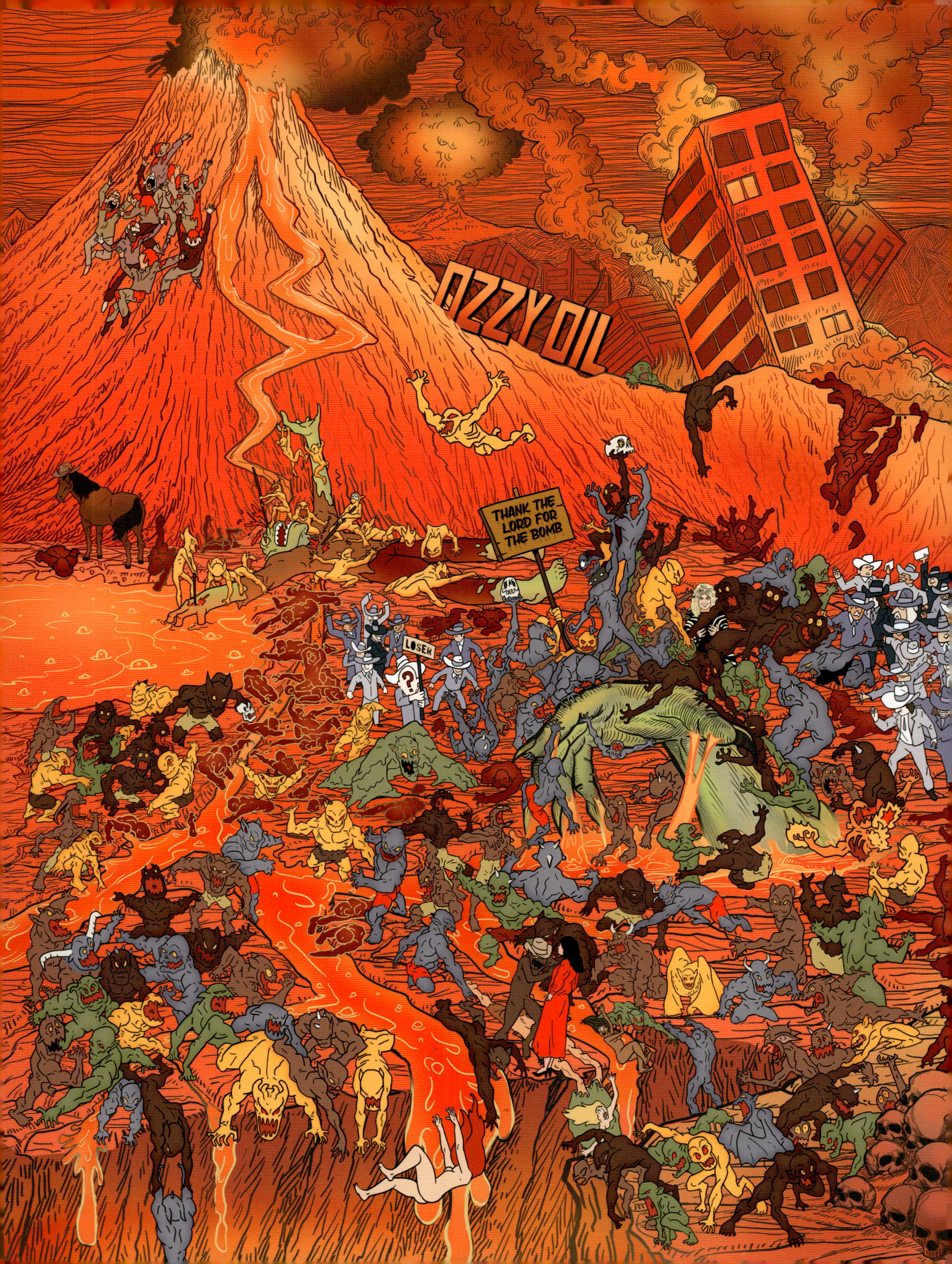
OZZY OIL
THANK THE LORD FOR THE BOMB
LOSER

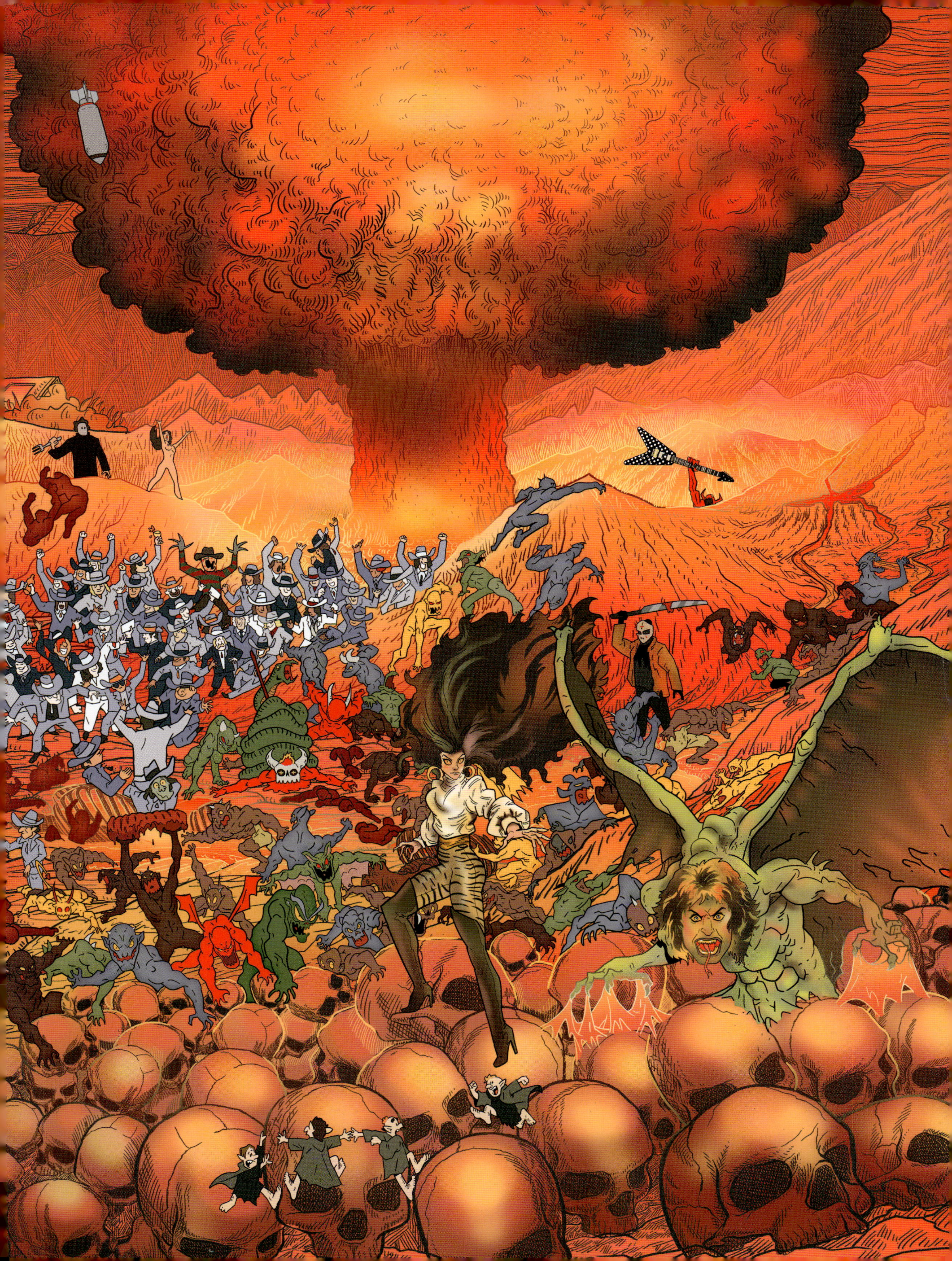

CAUTION
CAUTION
CAUTION
CAUTION
CAUTION
CAUTION
CAUTION
CAUTION
CAUTION
CAUTION

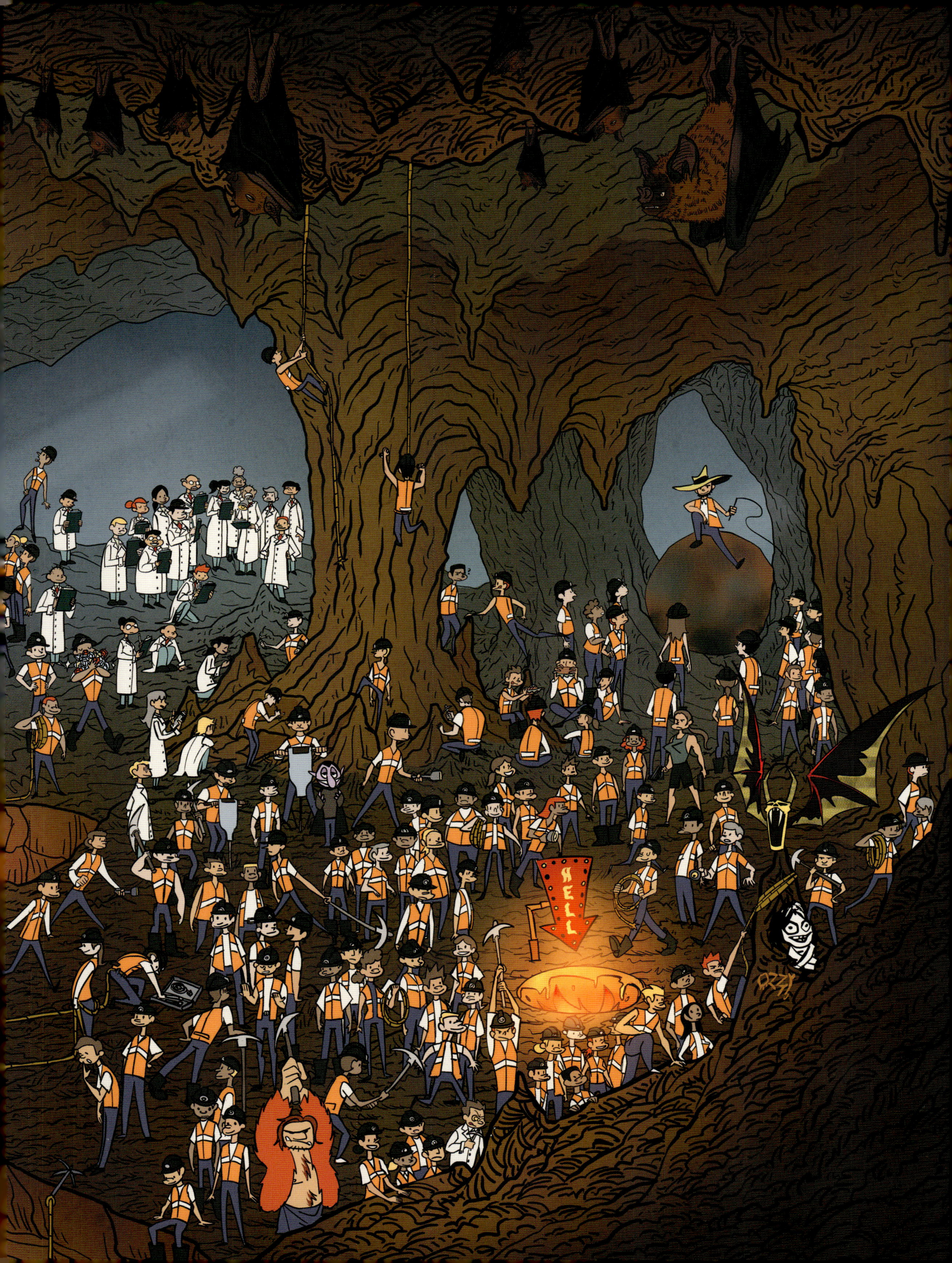
HELL

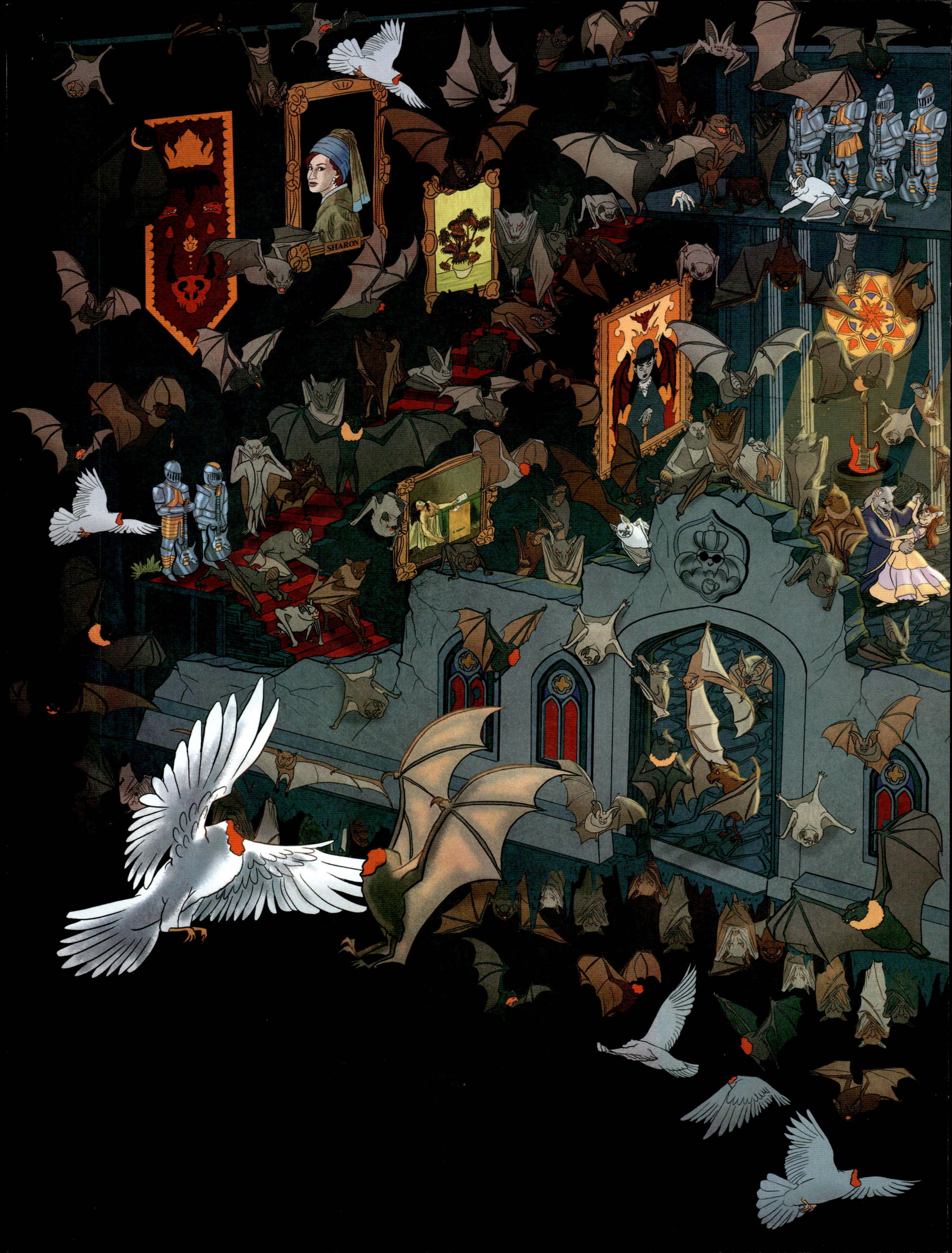
SHARON

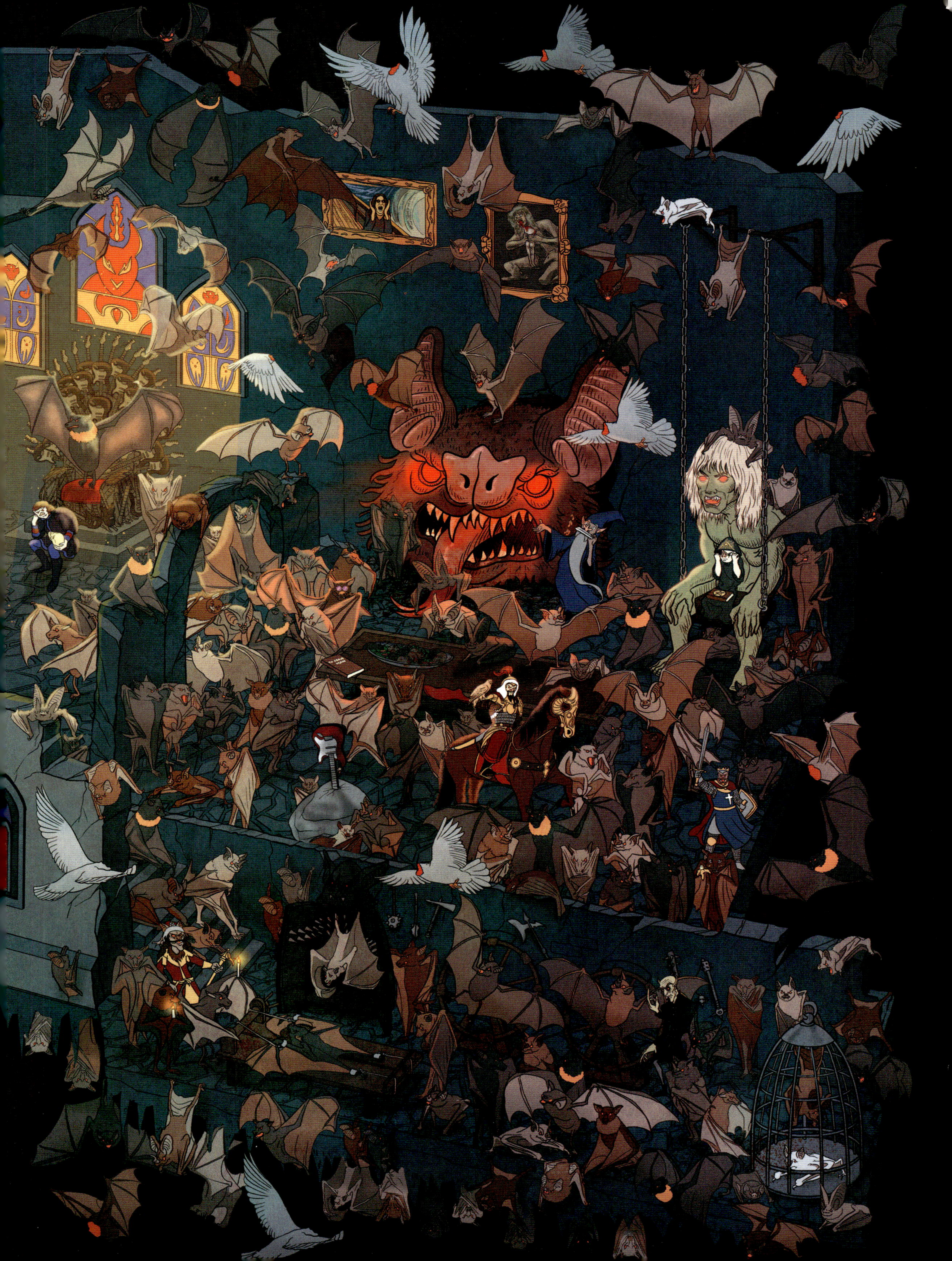

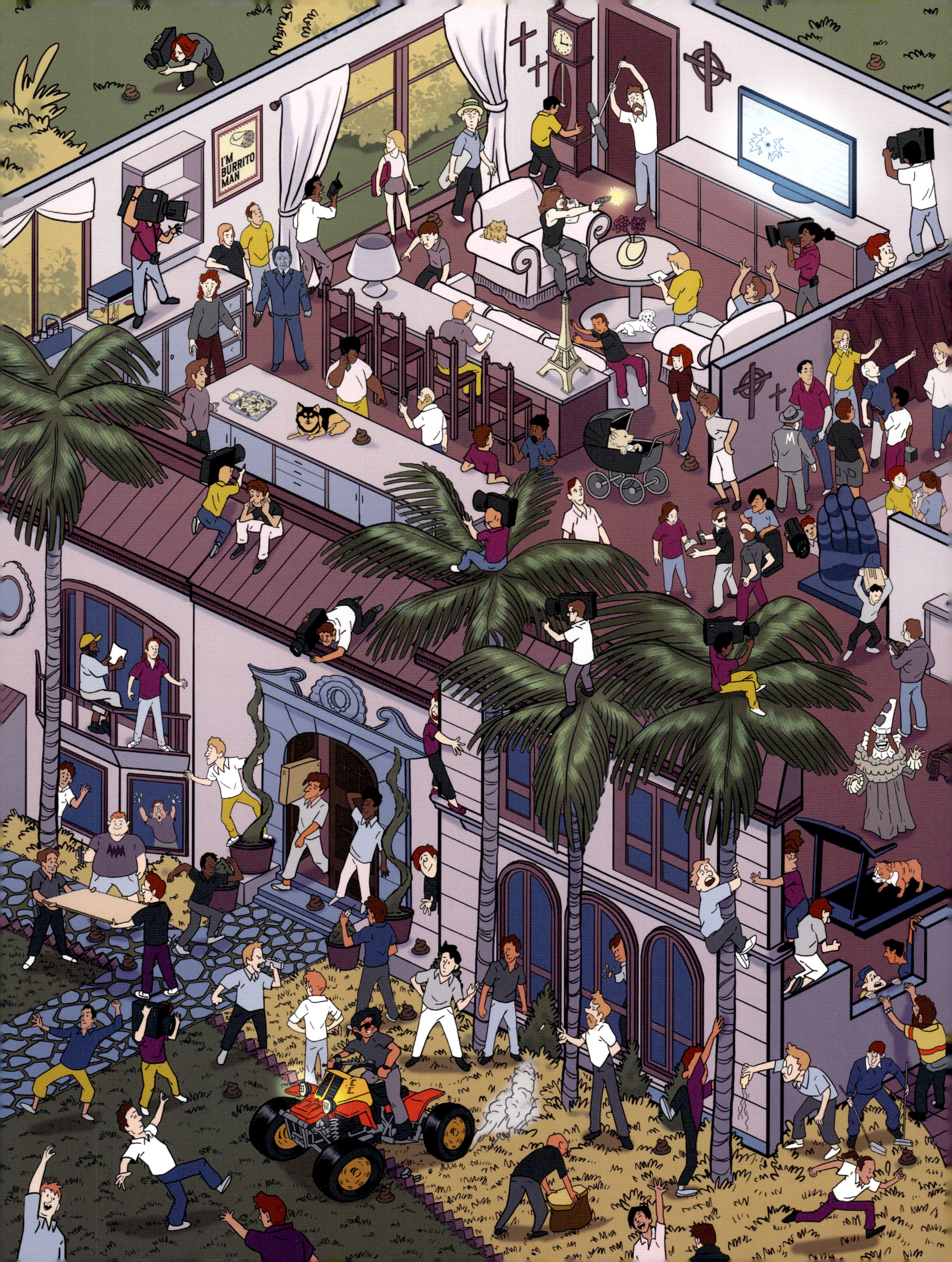
I'M BURRITO MAN

VOTE FOR JACK

STOP PREMATURE CHRISTMAS DECORATING!

BIG BROTHER IS WATCHING YOU

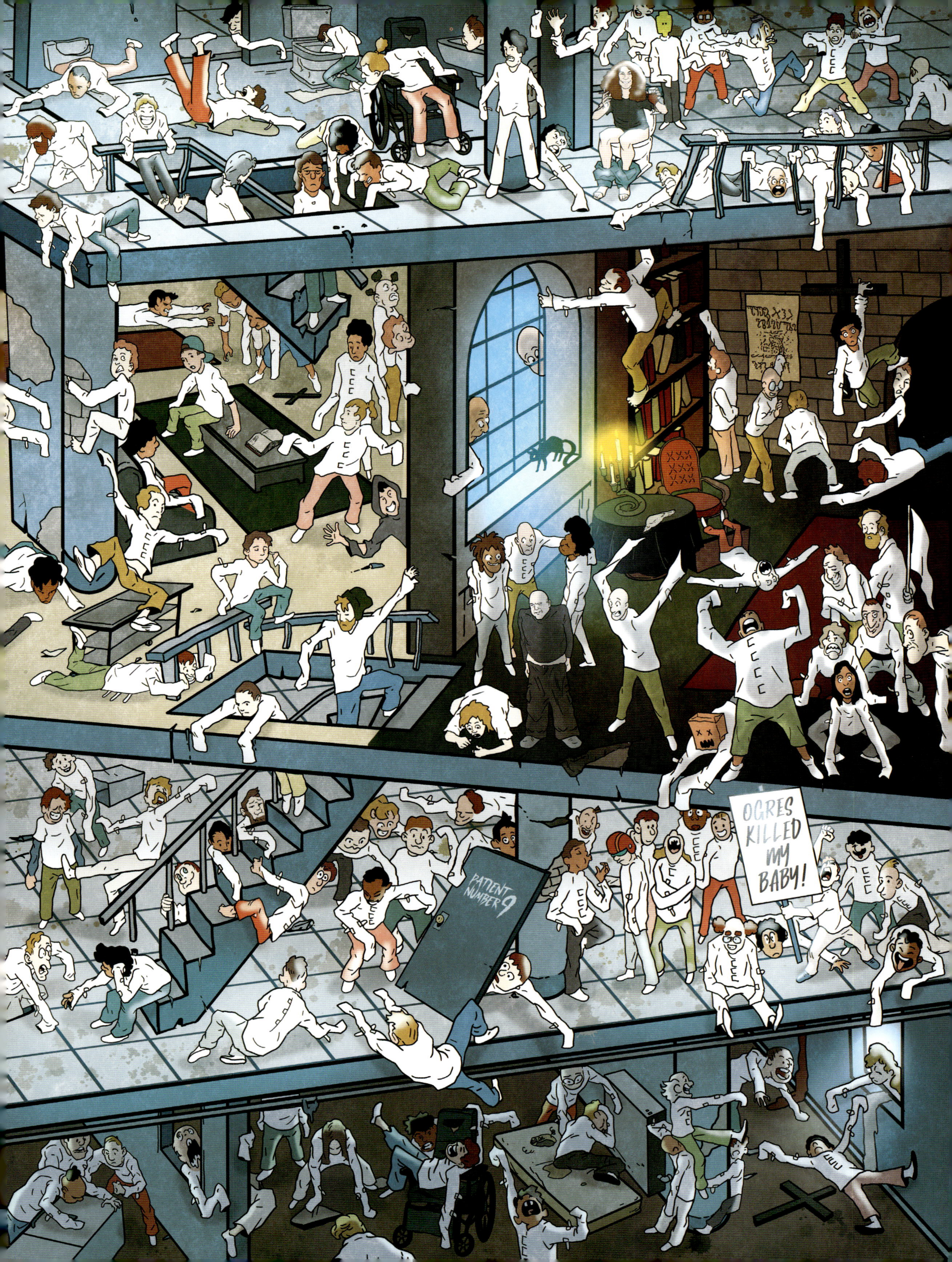
PATIENT NUMBER 9
OGRES KILLED MY BABY!

BREAKING NEWS

OZZY OSBOURNE
TOKYO 1964
LIVE AT BUDOKAN OZZY OSBOURNE
OZZY OSBOURNE

BIRMINGHAM

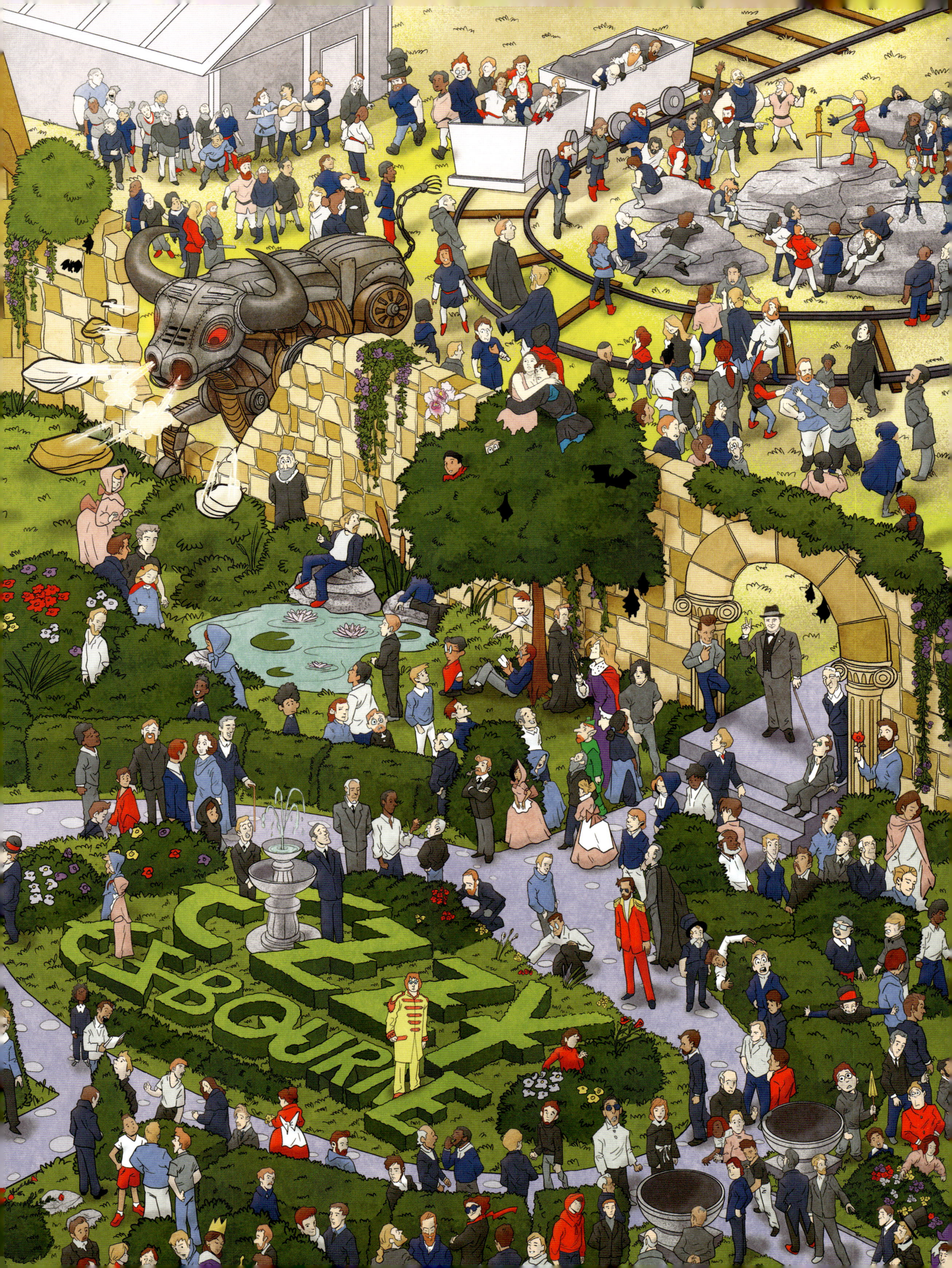

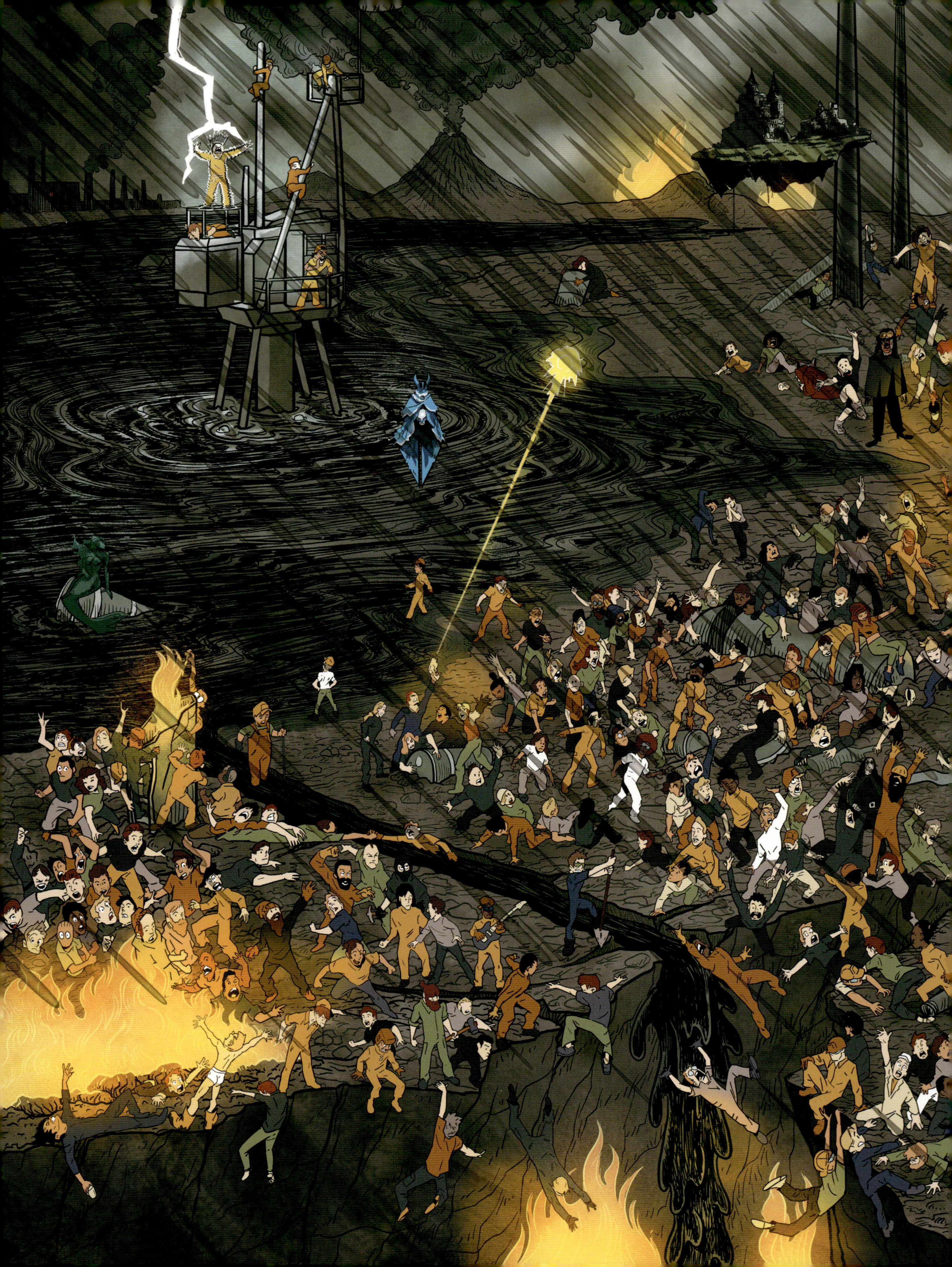

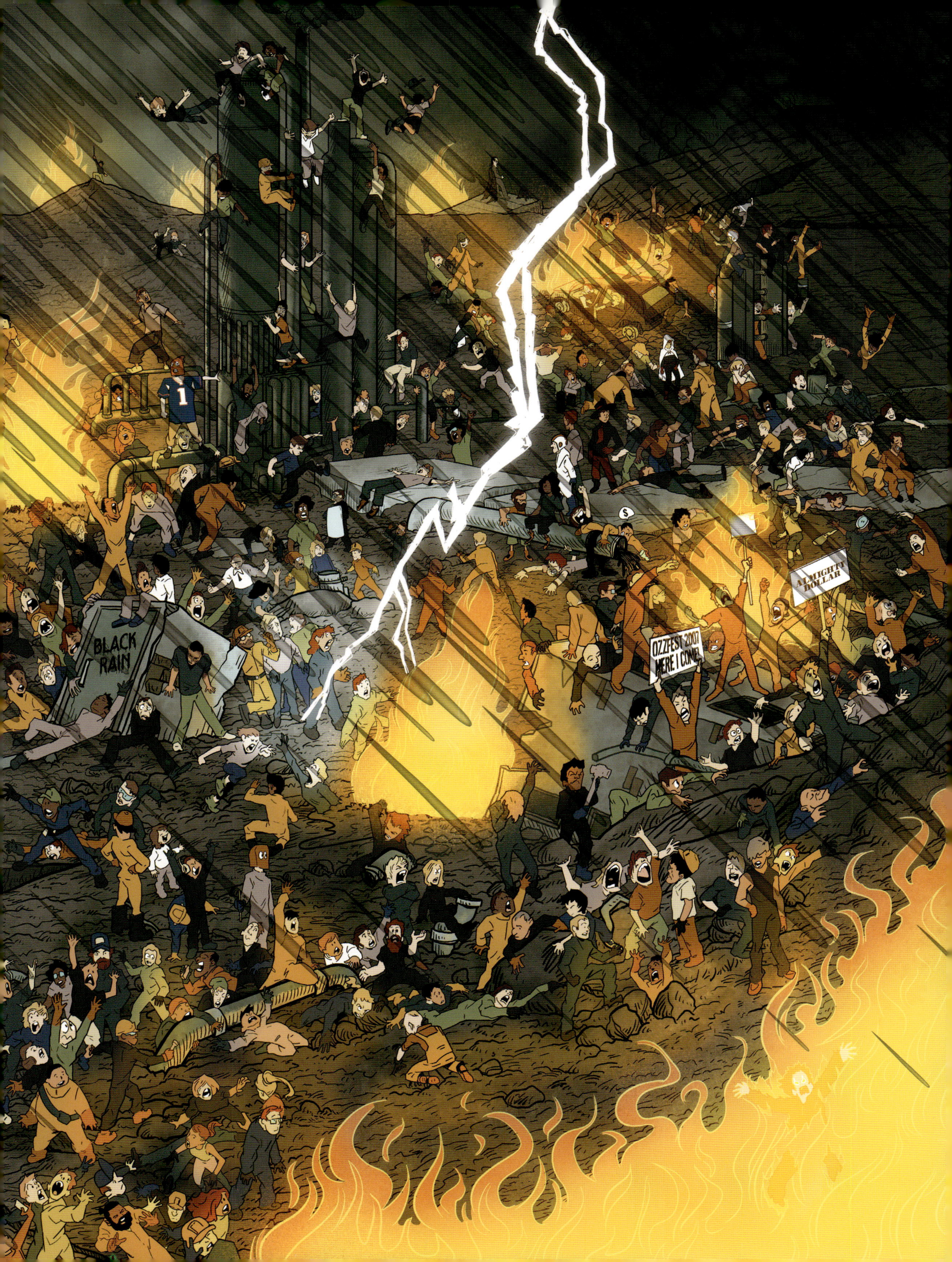
BLACK RAIN
OZZFEST 2007 HERE I COME!
ALMIGHTY DOLLAR

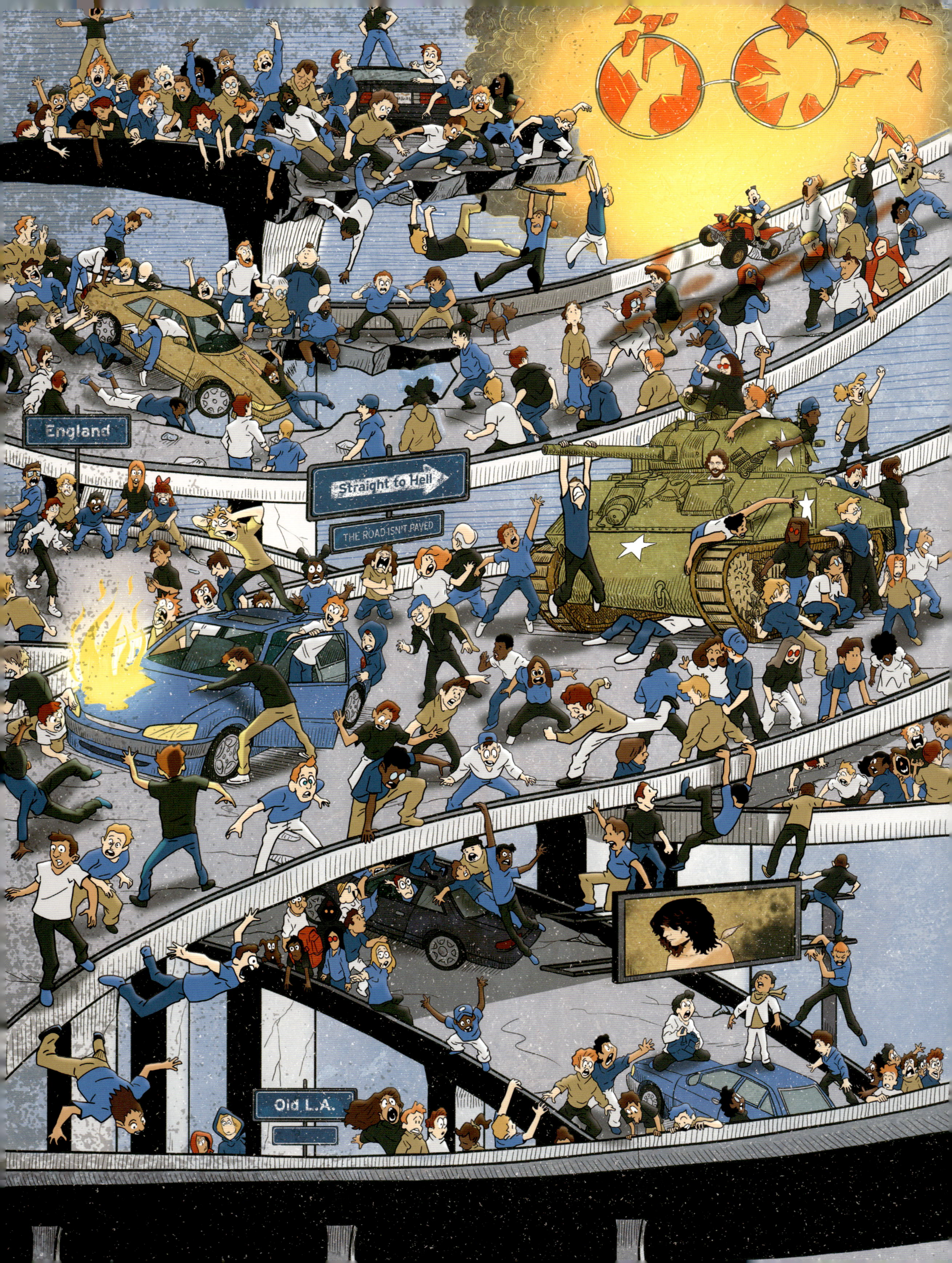
England
Straight to Hell
THE ROAD ISN'T PAVED
Old L.A.

Heaven
I'M GROUNDED FOR LIFE
NOW YOU'VE PISSED OFF GRANDMA !!!
The Devil IS MY BEST Friend
A HARD ROAD

THE "SUICIDE SOLUTION" CASE

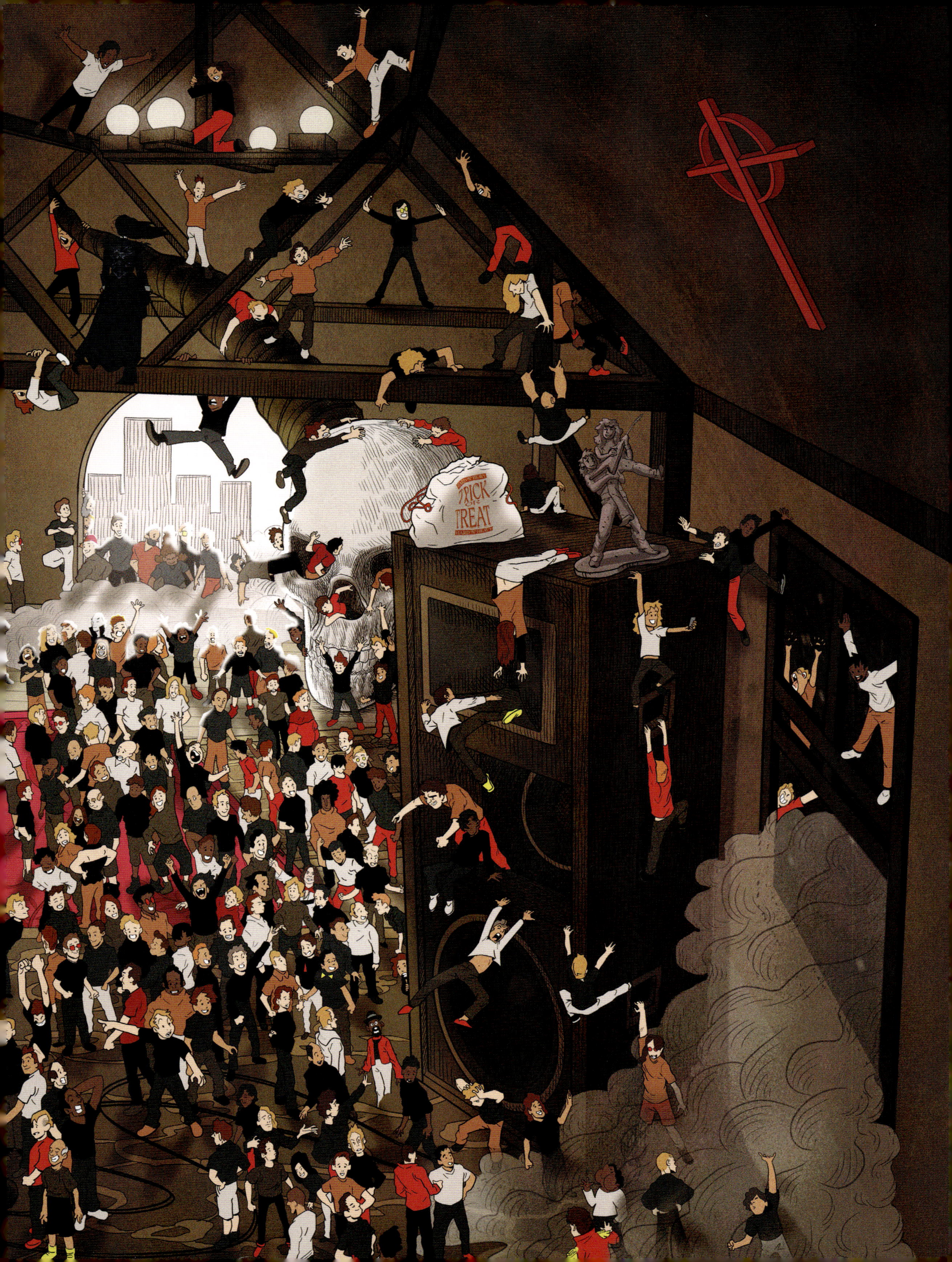
TRICK
OR
TREAT

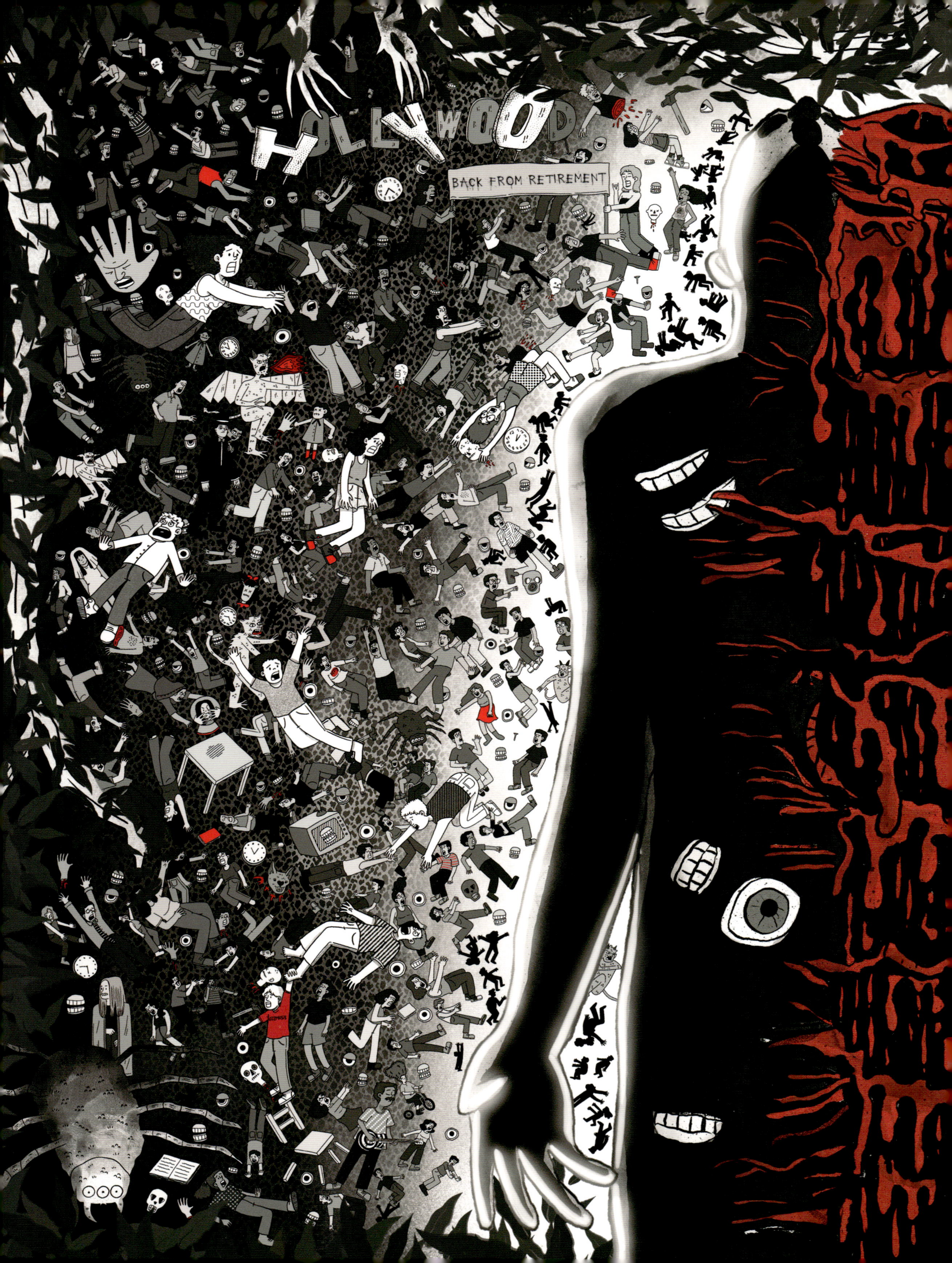
HOLLYWOOD
BACK FROM RETIREMENT

PASSION AND WARFARE